Church Chuckles

Tickling Your Holy Funny Bone

Publications International, Ltd.

Illustrator: Amanda Haley

Contributing Writers: Rebecca Christian, Kelly Cison, Lawrence Greenberg, Ellen Pill, Angela Sanchez, Terri Schlichenmeyer, Paul Seaburn, Kim Sloane, Carol Stigger, Niki Taylor, Lynda Twardowsky, Kathy Yonce

Louis Weber, CEO
Publications International, Ltd.
7373 North Cicero Avenue
Lincolnwood, Illinois 60712

ISBN-13: 978-1-4127-1769-4
ISBN-10: 1-4127-1769-8

Manufactured in USA.

8 7 6 5 4 3 2 1

Holy hilarity—who knew church could be so funny!

Laugh in church, and the church laughs with you ... cry, and you sit in the back with the babies. When it comes to bonding spiritually, breaking up can be as effective as breaking bread. Humor can be found every-where, in church signs, bulletin bloopers, Sunday school lessons—even the occasional sermon gaffe or the innocent words of a child. Share a spiritual laugh, and lift a spirit today.

3

Next Thursday there will be tryouts for the choir. Please come; they need all the help they can get.

Dear God,
Is the New Testament the upgrade of the old one?

Joey, age 8

❋ ❋ ❋

THIS WEEK'S SERMON

One of our assistant pastors stepped up to the podium to welcome a new family to the church. He declared the visitors "all most welcome," leaving the entire church wondering why this family was only "almost" welcome.

Sid's wedding was in less than a week, and he was feeling awful. He went to his minister for counsel. "I don't think I can go through with this," he said. "I am sick to my stomach, I can't sleep, and my legs are shaky and weak." The kindly minister smiled and said, "Don't worry, Sid, yours  are common symptoms. I have seen them quite often. You've got PMS."

"PMS?" said Sid, looking shocked.

"Yes," said his minister. "You have a classic case of Pre-Marriage Syndrome."

✳ ✳ ✳

"Forbidden fruit creates many jams."

AUTHOR UNKNOWN

Jorge had it figured out. "The father thought his boy might come back home. That's why he was called the Probable Son."

* * *

CHURCH NOTES

"Welcome, visitors!" the church bulletin read. "If you are visiting us today and if you are not afflicted with any church, please fill out the attached card, and our pastor will call on you."

* * *

In Wednesday's prayer group, Steve Phillips will read his speech "Loving One Another: Excepting Those of Other Cultures."

Sign above the door to the
church nursery:

> **"We shall not all
> sleep, but we shall
> all be changed."**
>
> 1 CORINTHIANS 15:51

The high school boys' youth group had gone camping in the mountains, where they found a spectacular clearing to set up their tents. They had a great evening of fellowship, Bible study, and worship with the youth pastor—truly a blessed night.

Early the next morning the youth pastor woke one of the older boys. "Anton, what do you see?"

"Wow, Pastor Joshua. I see the clearest sky I think I have ever seen, and look, is that an eagle?"

"Yes," said the pastor. "I think it is. What does all this make you think?"

"I'm thinking of God and all his majesty, and I'm thankful for this opportunity to experience it. How about you, Pastor?"

"Well, all of that, of course," the pastor answered. "But I also have to notice that someone stole our tent."

Jesus was making his usual rounds in heaven when he noticed a white-haired man sitting in a corner looking disconsolate. The next week he was disturbed to come across him again, looking equally miserable, and a week later he stopped to talk to him.

"See here, dear man," said Jesus kindly, "this is heaven. The sun is shining, you have all you could want to eat, all the instruments you might want to play—you're supposed to be blissfully happy! What's wrong?"

"Well," said the old man, "you see, I was a carpenter on earth, and lost my only, dearly beloved son at an early age. And here in heaven I was hoping more than anything to find him."

Tears sprang from Jesus' eyes. "Father!" he cried.

The old man jumped to his feet, burst into tears, and choked, "PINOCCHIO?"

Bobby knew exactly what Jesus would drive: "A van that seats 12 and can pull a boat."

✳ ✳ ✳

CHURCH HAPPENINGS

Ladies, don't forget the rummage sale. It is a good chance to get rid of those things not worth keeping around the house. Bring your husbands.

One day Eve called out to God from the Garden of Eden, "God, I have a problem."

"What's the problem, Eve?"

"Lord, you've created me and provided this beautiful spot, these wonderful animals, and that goofy snake, but I'm just not happy."

"Why is that, Eve?" came the voice from above.

"Lord, I am lonely. And I'm sick to death of apples."

"Well, perhaps I have a solution. I shall create a man for you to keep you company."

"Oh, thank you," cried Eve. "But is there a catch?"

"Yes, well, there is one," God answered. "You'll have to let him believe that I made him first."

My biggest fear is going to heaven and seeing God wearing a wristband that says, "I don't know. What would you do?"

✳ ✳ ✳

THIS WEEK'S SERMON

There's a sign-up sheet for anyone wishing to be baptized on the table in the foyer.

A taxi driver and a pastor arrive at the Pearly Gates at the same time, and St. Peter greets the taxi driver warmly. A stretch limo pulls up to the gate. The driver steps out, places a beautiful silken robe on the taxi driver, holds the door while he gets in the back, then drives him to a mansion. The pastor is excited. If a taxi driver gets all that, he can only imagine what his reward for a life of service to the Lord will be.

But the next car he sees is a Ford Pinto. A driver steps out of the car, tosses a terry cloth robe and the keys to the pastor, and walks back through the gates.

"There must be some mistake," the pastor exclaims. "I served the Lord faithfully for over 40 years. That was a taxi driver. Are you sure there wasn't a mix-up?"

"Oh no," St. Peter replies. "You see, while you worked, people slept. While the taxi driver worked, people prayed."

OUR CHURCH TODAY

Emily attended church with her grandmother for the first time. Before the service, her grandmother gave her $1 to put in the offering plate. But when the ushers passed the plate, Emily didn't give them the money. When her grandmother asked why, Emily said, "My dad says you don't have to tip if you don't get good service!"

✳ ✳ ✳

CHURCH NOTES

The concert held in the Fellowship Hall was a great success. Special thanks are due to the minister's daughter Ann, who labored the whole evening at the piano, which as usual fell upon her.

As a newly born-again Christian, the barber did not want to waste any time in sharing his faith with everyone possible. When the very first customer came in for a shave Monday morning, the barber got him all lathered up and then, walking toward him with the razor, asked, "Are you prepared to meet God?" The frightened man jumped up and ran from the shop, never to be seen there again.

✳ ✳ ✳

Dear God,
When exactly will hell freeze over? My dad said that's about the time I'll get my new pony.

Tricia, age 10

* * *

A well-known minister was invited to speak at a city council meeting on a Friday afternoon, since he was in town to preach all weekend. Knowing he would be repeating some of the same jokes during the Sunday sermons, he requested the newspaper reporter in attendance not include them in her article. On Saturday morning, there was a nice write-up about the visiting minister, with this unfortunate ending: "The minister told a number of funny stories that we simply could not publish."

You may not be spending enough time reading your Bible if you think the Minor Prophets were all underage.

* * *

Tomas was a very bright little eight-year-old, but his Sunday school teacher could not seem to get him to concentrate on the lessons being taught. He always wound up turning his lesson sheet over and drawing trucks, cars, and planes. During the spring season, when the Easter story was being taught, Tomas really seemed to be paying attention. He even raised his hand and asked how to spell an important name from the story, so his teacher was interested to look at his paper as he left the class.

And there on the back of the lesson page was a picture of a jet, with a man waving out the front window. Underneath the plane in Tomas's careful handwriting was a caption that read "Pontius the Pilate."

After watching the pope on TV, Joanna wondered, "If the pope rides in a Popemobile, did Jesus ride in a Chrysler?"

✳ ✳ ✳

Seen in the Christmas pageant program:

THE THREE WISE MEN:

Harold Aimly and Brian Howell

As Shane and his wife were driving home from church one week, she mentioned, "Cindy sure is putting on the weight. Do you think she's pregnant?"

"I didn't notice, dear."

"Well, did you see how short Diane's skirt was? And at her age."

"I'm sorry, dear, I didn't notice."

"Surely you noticed the way the Smiths let their kids crawl all over everything during fellowship?"

"No, dear, I'm sorry, I guess I didn't notice that either."

"Honestly, Shane, I don't even know why you go to church anymore!"

✳ ✳ ✳

"Jesus saves...passes to Moses...shoots...scores!"

AUTHOR UNKNOWN

Dear God,
Why is Sunday school on Sunday? I thought it was supposed to be our day of rest.

Andrea, age 6

* * *

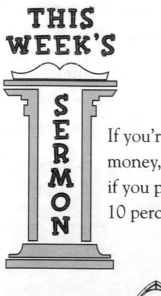

THIS WEEK'S SERMON

If you're going to pray for money, we'd appreciate if you pray for an extra 10 percent.

Gracie was really learning a lot in Sunday school every week, and she convinced her dad it was important to say a blessing before eating dinner. One night Gracie's parents were arguing something terrible before dinner. When they sat down to eat, Gracie's father used a pleasant voice to say the blessing. Gracie

was silent a little while and then asked, "Daddy, do you think God hears us when we pray?" Her father assured her that he did think so.

"And do you think God hears us the rest of the time also?" Gracie asked. Her father said yes to this as well.

"Well, Daddy, which do you think he believes?"

After the church service, Billy told the pastor, "When I grow up, I'm going to give you some money. My daddy says you're one of the poorest preachers we've ever had."

✳ ✳ ✳

OUR CHURCH TODAY

It's not that I mind the taste of communion wafers. I'm just wondering why no one has thought to add salt.

Moses and Jesus were playing golf. On the first hole was a long fairway with a water hazard. Moses said, "Jesus, we should tee off from the novice tees. We can't make it over the water from here."

Jesus replied, "Arnold Palmer made a shot from here. If he can do it, so can I."

Jesus drove his ball toward the green. It sailed out over the water and fell in. Moses sighed, walked toward the water, parted it, and retrieved Jesus' ball.

"Jesus," Moses tried again. "We should tee off from up there. We can't make it from here. If you try that again and your ball falls in the water, I won't get it."

But Jesus insisted. "Arnold Palmer made a shot from here. If he can do it, so can I."

Jesus again drove his ball toward the green. It sailed out over the water and once again fell in. Jesus headed down to the water hazard and then walked on the water to where his ball had fallen in.

Moses was waiting at the tee when the next foursome came through and witnessed Jesus walking on water.

"Holy mackerel!" one of them exclaimed. "Does that guy think he's Jesus?"

"No," Moses answered. "He thinks he's Arnold Palmer."

❋ ❋ ❋

CHURCH NOTES

ATTENTION: The bowl at the back of the church marked "For the sick" is for monetary donations only.

THIS WEEK'S

"Let us bow our heads in prayer for the many who are sick of our church and community."

✳ ✳ ✳

Dear Pastor,
I would like to go to heaven one day because I know my brother won't be there.

Angela, age 8

The minister approached a very wealthy member of the congregation, a man who had attended for years but had never tithed nor contributed in any way. The minister began to make a case for great need in the church and what a blessing it was to give to God's work.

"I understand everything you're saying, Reverend," the man answered. "But perhaps there are some things about me that you don't know. For instance, my mother is quite ill and requires a full-time nurse. My sister and her husband died, leaving four young children as orphans. My own son is in a remote area of Africa, where he teaches medicine to the natives and receives no pay or support from anyone."

The minister was ashamed; he hadn't known any of that.

"And if I don't send any of them a penny," the man continued, "why would I help you?"

✳ ✳ ✳

The Sunday school teacher had spent three weeks teaching the story of the prodigal son to her second grade class. She wanted to make sure the children understood every important point of the story, including the resentful brother, the loving and forgiving father, and so on. As she was quizzing her class, she came to this question: "Now children, out of all the characters in the story, who was not at all happy to see the prodigal son returning home?"

"I know, I know," shouted sweet little Marianna. "It was the fatted calf."

28

The pastor was growing a bit tired of eating leftovers for dinner. One night they sat down to leftovers again, and the wife was stunned to notice her husband begin to poke around at his meal without saying grace.

"Dear! Aren't you going to offer thanks before we eat?"

He put down his fork and sighed. "If you can point out one thing on this plate I haven't already said thanks for at least twice this week, I'll be glad to."

※　※　※

Dusty Bibles

lead to dirty lives.

The Sunday school teacher was nervous about teaching the upcoming lesson on hell. She was afraid it would scare her nine- and ten-year-old students.

"Today we are going to talk about hell," she told them. "What do you know about it?"

Paul raised his hand eagerly. "I don't know where it is, but my mama is always telling my daddy he should go there."

✳ ✳ ✳

"In the beginning there was nothing and God said 'Let there be light,' and there was still nothing but everybody could see it."

DAVE THOMAS

CHURCH

Barbara Green remains in the hospital and needs blood donors for another transfusion. She is also having trouble sleeping and requests tapes of Pastor Jack's sermons.

❋ ❋ ❋

VOLUNTEER OPPORTUNITIES

The choir is sponsoring a canned goods drive. Please participate and bring your can to church.

Seen on a bumper sticker:

Drive carefully. It's not only cars that can be recalled by their maker.

❋ ❋ ❋

CHURCH

N
E
W
S

The power went out at St. Mary's during Father Jim's sermon last week, causing Mass confusion.

OUR CHURCH TODAY

Our pastor had been asked a few times if spouses had called him to "tell" on them, because it seemed as though the sermons were directed straight at them. One particular sermon really had a few of the church members feeling convicted, and the pastor, sensing this, decided to end with this statement: "All sinners referred to in my sermon are purely fictitious. Any similarity to members of this congregation, past or present, is strictly confidential. I mean coincidental!"

❋ ❋ ❋

A Sunday school teacher asked his class, "Does anyone know what we mean by sins of omission?" One of the girls replied, "Aren't those the sins we could have committed but didn't?"

Two little boys, ages eight and ten, were always getting into trouble, and their parents didn't know what to do about it. When they heard that a preacher in town had been successful in  disciplining children, the boys' mother asked if he would speak with her boys. The preacher agreed, but he asked to see them individually.

The mother sent the eight-year-old in first. The preacher, a large man with a booming voice, sat the younger boy down and asked him sternly, "Do you know where God is, son?" The boy's mouth dropped open, and he made no response.

The preacher repeated the question in an even sterner tone, "Where is God?" Again, the boy made no attempt to answer. The preacher looked him squarely in the eyes and said again, "Where is God?"

The boy screamed and bolted from the room. When his older brother saw him, he asked, "What happened?"

The younger brother, gasping for breath, replied, "We are in BIG trouble this time. God is missing, and they think we did it!"

✳ ✳ ✳

CHURCH NOTES

The Ladies Society will be selling its new cookbook at the church supper this Wednesday night. The proceeds will help purchase a stomach pump for our community hospital.

The French gentleman often sat in the front of the church, taking up the whole row. The other parishoners referred to him as Pepe La Pew.

✳ ✳ ✳

Dear God,
I know why Noah didn't take any pets on the ark. Because it was already raining cats and dogs.

Antonio, age 9

As Christmas approached, Liam drew a picture of the manger scene with all of the traditional characters, plus one—a fourth wise man, and a chubby one at that. "And who is that, Liam?" his teacher asked.

"That's Round John Virgin," he replied.

My husband is our church's senior pastor, and the last time he was leaving to lead a mission trip he sat our young children down and talked to them about the type of behavior he expected from them while he was away. One point he stressed was that they were all to sleep in their own beds and not sneak into ours, as they had a habit of doing. On the Sunday morning he returned, we met him at the church, and the children ran up to him in the midst of a crowd of congregants. "Daddy, you're going to be so happy! No one slept with Mommy while you were gone!"

✳ ✳ ✳

CHURCH NOTES

Latecomers are asked to wait until the service is over to be seated.

Trouble sleeping?

We have sermons—

come hear one!

※ ※ ※

At the offering, Reverend Ellen reminded the congregation, "We do accept checks and credit cards, even though they don't say 'In God We Trust.'"

George was spending Friday night and all day Saturday with his grandmother in the country, and it had snowed overnight. Grandma couldn't wait to bundle up George and take him walking in the beautiful, fresh snow.

"Isn't it wonderful, George? Doesn't it seem like our Lord has painted this gorgeous scenery, just for us to enjoy this morning?"

"Yes, Grandma! And do you want to know what makes it even better? God had to do this all with his left hand!"

Grandma didn't have any idea what George meant.

"Grandma," he explained patiently. "Don't you know that Jesus sits on the right hand of God?"

※　※　※

Libby was so happy with her report card, she let everyone in church know about it by singing "Amazing Grades."

Reverend Larry pleaded with the congregation to dig deeper for the offering. "Drawing a halo over Abe Lincoln's head doesn't make the five go any further."

❋ ❋ ❋

OUR CHURCH TODAY

Asked how the membership drive was going, Reverend Phil said, "Many are called, but pews are open."

❋ ❋ ❋

"Most of us spend the first six days of each week sowing wild oats, then we go to church on Sunday and pray for a crop failure."

FRED ALLEN

Karen's grandfather was a minister, and her grandmother served chicken so often that her grandfather called it The Gospel Bird. One day Karen asked her grandmother why she served it almost every Sunday. Her grandmother answered, "Well, in case your grandfather goes on and on, it's the only thing that tastes better the longer it stews."

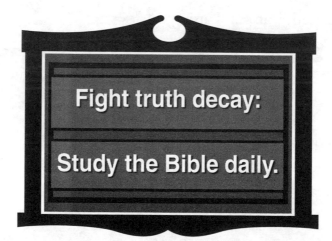

Fight truth decay:

Study the Bible daily.

A minister tells of his first Sunday in a new congregation, when he was presenting the children's message. The sanctuary in the new church featured magnificent stained glass windows, so his message centered on how each of us is called to help make up the whole picture of life (the life of the community of the faithful). He explained that, like the pictures  in the windows, it takes many little panels of glass to make the whole picture. "You see, each one of you is a little pane." And then, pointing to each child, "You're a little pane. And you're a little pane. And you're a little pane. And..." It took a few moments before the minister realized why the children looked so hurt.

A staunchly Baptist couple decided it was important that the pet they own be equally religious. They found a dog they liked and were delighted to find it was very well trained. When they asked the dog to fetch the Bible, it did so immediately. When they asked it to turn to Psalm 23, the dog used its paws with great dexterity to obey quickly. They were impressed, purchased the animal, and went home.

That night they invited friends over so they could show off their new pet. The friends were also quite impressed, and they asked whether the dog was able to do any of the usual dog tricks as  well. This stopped the couple cold, as they hadn't thought about it doing "normal" tricks.

They called the dog over and said, "Roll over." The dog promptly rolled over. It proved it could

sit up and shake hands as well, so they kept going. The man stood up and said, "Heel!"

Immediately, the dog jumped up on the couch, put its right paw on the woman's forehead, closed its eyes in concentration, and bowed its head.

They had been deceived! The dog was Pentecostal!

※　※　※

OUR CHURCH TODAY

Everyone wanted Father John to get a new sound system, but he knew that the feedback was the only thing keeping many parishioners awake during his sermons.

An elderly priest was dying, so he sent for two members of his parish: one an IRS agent, the other a lawyer. When they arrived, they were each asked by a nun to sit in a chair on either side of his bed. The priest gave a faint smile when he knew they were both there, and he settled in for what would be his last night on earth.

By morning, the priest had passed on to his reward. As the two men were preparing to leave, the lawyer asked the nun why they had been called, since neither had been a close friend of the priest.

"Oh, I suppose it would be all right to tell you," the nun said. "Father said that Jesus had died between two thieves and he wanted to do the same."

✳ ✳ ✳

The Reverend Merriwether spoke briefly, much to the delight of the congregation.

CHURCH NOTES

Brother Lamar has gone on to be the Lord.

✳ ✳ ✳

The minister had given a stirring message about the blessing of forgiving others based on the forgiveness we have so freely received. "Who here is ready to pray with me to forgive all those who have sinned against them?" asked the minister. Everyone but one elderly woman raised their hand. "Miss Lucy, please, tell us why it is you feel you don't have anyone to forgive?"

Miss Lucy replied, "Because I have outlived all those heathen sinners, that's why!"

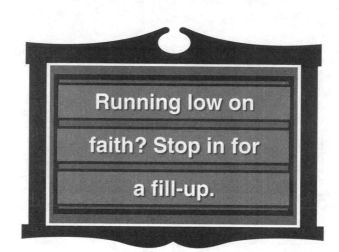

Running low on
faith? Stop in for
a fill-up.

✳ ✳ ✳

One evening Pastor Steve asked how many had followed his instructions of the past week and read Mark 17, and every hand went up. The pastor said, "Mark has only 16 chapters. Let me begin my sermon on the sin of lying."

As the Sunday school teacher described how Lot's wife looked back and was turned into a pillar of salt, James interrupted: "My mommy looked back once while she was driving, and she turned into a telephone pole!"

✳ ✳ ✳

Dear God,
I didn't think orange went with purple until I saw the sunset you made on Tuesday. That was cool!

Sean, age 9

Arthur was sitting outside the local pub one day, quietly enjoying a pint, when a nun suddenly appeared at his table and began decrying the evils of drink.

"You should be ashamed of yourself, young man. Drinking is a sin. Alcohol is the blood of the devil."

Arthur protested, "How do you know that, Sister?"

"Mother Superior told me so."

"But have you ever had a drink yourself? How can you be sure you're right?"

"Don't be ridiculous," the nun said indignantly. "Of course I have never had a sip of liquor in my life."

"Then let me buy you a drink," Arthur offered. "And if you still believe it's evil I will give up drink for life."

"How could I, a nun, sit outside this public house drinking?"

"I'll get the barkeep to put it in a teacup for you. No one will know it's not tea."

The nun reluctantly agreed, so Arthur went inside to the bar.

"Another pint for me, and a triple vodka on the rocks. And could you put the vodka in a teacup?"

"Ah," the bartender nodded knowingly. "It's that drunken nun again, is it?"

✳ ✳ ✳

Sign at a church cemetery:

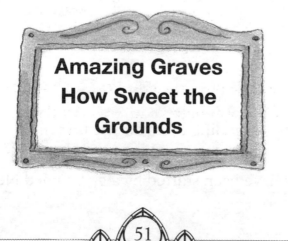

**Amazing Graves
How Sweet the
Grounds**

Three buddies die in a car crash, and they go to heaven.

There, they are all asked, "When you are in your casket and your friends are mourning, what would you like to hear them say about you?"

The first guy says, "I would like to hear them say that I was a great doctor and a great family man."

The second guy says, "I would like to hear that I was a wonderful husband and schoolteacher who made a huge difference in the children of tomorrow."

The last guy replies, "I would like to hear them say, 'Look! He's moving!'"

✳ ✳ ✳

After attending Mass for the first time, Megan decided that the Catholic church must have been started by a guy named Neil.

An ordained minister was stationed aboard a U.S. Navy battleship. He was concerned about the morale of some of the sailors after the announcements he heard on his first Sunday morning aboard: "Religious services commencing. Maintain silence about the decks. Knock off all unnecessary work." An hour later this announcement followed: "Resume all unnecessary work."

✳ ✳ ✳

Hannah always behaves beautifully at Sunday school; however, she gets a bit fidgety when her parents linger in the Fellowship Hall too long. "Mommy, why do we have to sit here so long?" she asked one week.

"Daddy has to drink enough coffee to wake up for the drive home, dear."

CHURCH HAPPENINGS

A songfest will be hell at the Methodist church Wednesday.

✳ ✳ ✳

A preacher ended his temperance sermon by saying, "The world would be a better place if everyone poured their beer, wine, and whiskey into the river." Then he sat down. The song leader stood and announced with a smile, "For our closing song, let us sing Hymn 365: 'Shall We Gather at the River.'"

The first commandment was when Eve told Adam to eat the apple.

＊ ＊ ＊

At the end of vacation Bible camp, each child was asked to tell about his or her favorite Bible story. When five-year-old Parker was called on, he stood up to share about Daniel in the lion's den.

"Well," he said, "the king was mad at Daniel, because Daniel kept praying to the true God, and the king said Daniel had to go in the lion's den."

The teacher was very pleased that Parker had learned so well.

But Parker continued, "The lion was going to eat Daniel, but then God put a thorn in the lion's paw and Daniel pulled it out, and then they become best friends, so Daniel stayed alive until the morning."

Mary loved to cook, and food was her ministry. In fact, it was her job to organize the weekly Wonderful Wednesday supper, a meal held in the church basement for all church volunteers.

When the new pastor arrived, among the changes he instituted was a policy of no desserts at Wonderful Wednesdays during Lent. Mary, who loved indulging people's sweet tooths, reluctantly quit making her usual pies and cakes and instead began to offer vanilla pudding with fruit in it, which she called "fruit salad."

When the pastor observed that it certainly seemed more like a dessert than a salad, Mary told him firmly, "Desperate times require desperate measures. If Jesus could turn water into wine, I can turn pudding into salad."

Feeling in the dark?

Follow the Son.

✳ ✳ ✳

A nun who worked for the Visiting Angels was out making her rounds when she ran out of gas. Luckily, she was less than a block from a gas station. Realizing she didn't have a gas can, she looked through her trunk for something that would hold enough gas to get her back to the station to fill up. All she could find was a bedpan she was delivering to one of her patients. The nun carried the bedpan to the station, filled it with gas, walked carefully back to the car, and was pouring the gas into the tank when a man walked by.

"Now that's what I call faith!" the man said.

"I hope I get to the Pearly Gates before Daddy does," said Lana. "He's always losing our gate opener."

The Pearly Gates

✳ ✳ ✳

God noticed that Adam was lonely. He said to him, "Adam, I am going to give you the perfect companion. She's great fun, and she will help you out around the garden. She's everything you ever wanted."

Adam replied, "What will she cost me?"

"An arm and a leg," God answered.

Shocked, Adam said, "Well, what can I get for a rib?"

After a very long and boring sermon, the parishioners filed out of the church, saying nothing to the preacher. Toward the end of the line was a thoughtful woman who always commented on the sermons. Today she chose her words carefully and said, "Pastor, your sermon reminded me of the peace and love of God."

The pastor was thrilled. "No one has ever said anything like that about my preaching before. Please, tell me why you felt that way."

"It reminded me of the peace of God because it passed all understanding, and the love of God because it endured forever!"

✳ ✳ ✳

ACKNOWLEDGMENTS

A new loudspeaker system has been installed in the church. It was given by one of our members in honor of his wife.

59

A priest, a pastor, and a rabbi all served as chaplains in the armed services, and under the duress of wartime they made a wild bet with each other. When they got back stateside, they would each find a grizzly bear and attempt to convert it to their religion.

The priest and pastor were called to a Veterans Hospital some years later, where they found their friend the rabbi in terrible condition, with IVs and wires everywhere, and in a body cast. He seemed asleep, so they began to quietly catch up on their lives. Of course, the bet came up. The priest had found a bear, and as soon as he got close enough, he sprinkled it with holy water, tossed a communion wafer into its mouth, and read to it from the catechism. The pastor had

had equal success with the bear he found. He had tricked the bear into slipping in a creek, where he quickly dunked its head under for a baptism, immediately gave it a nice casserole for its first potluck, and read to it from the Bible. As they were congratulating each other, the rabbi opened his eyes. He had been listening the whole time. "I suppose circumcision may not have been the best place for me to start," he said.

✳ ✳ ✳

Where will you spend eternity? Smoking or nonsmoking?

Three doctors are waiting in line at the Pearly Gates. St. Peter walks out and asks the first one, "What have you done to deserve entrance into heaven?"

"I am an obstetrician and have brought thousands of the Lord's babies into the world."

"Good enough to enter the gates," replied St. Peter, and in the obstetrician goes. The same question is asked of the second doctor. "I am a general practitioner and go to developing countries three times a year to cure the poor."

St. Peter is impressed and allows her through the gates.

The third doctor steps up in line and, knowing the question, blurts out, "I am the director of an HMO."

St. Peter thinks about this for a while, then says, "Okay, you can enter heaven ... but only for two days."

✳ ✳ ✳

CHURCH NOTES

The Women's Association still needs more crotch pot recipes for the cookbook they are compiling.

✳ ✳ ✳

As he went out to play, Aaron had this thought: "Poor Jesus probably never got invited to play hide-and-seek because he always knew where everyone was hiding."

A pastor and his administrative assistant were returning from a conference when his car broke down. The town they were towed to had one motel, which had one room available. "Angela, I believe the Lord will understand these awkward circumstances. I will sleep on the couch, and you may have the bed."

As it turned out, the heat was broken in the room, and Angela was freezing. "Pastor, I am freezing over here." The pastor went to the closet and got her an extra blanket. About ten minutes later came the same complaint. Again, the pastor got up and got his secretary another blanket. This was not enough to warm her up, and she soon said, "Pastor, I can't stop shivering."

The pastor replied, completely out of character, "You know, Angela, I think the Lord would understand and forgive me if I acted as though you were my wife tonight." Angela was shocked, and she began protesting just as the pastor continued, "Why don't you get up and get your own blanket this time?"

People are like tea bags. You have to put them in hot water before you know how strong they are.

❋ ❋ ❋

CHURCH NOTES

Gambling can ruin your life. Let the church help.

❋ ❋ ❋

"Don't question God, for He may reply: 'If you're so anxious for answers, come up here.'"

AUTHOR UNKNOWN

Bobby's mother worked with him for several weeks, helping him memorize his poem for the church's annual Christmas program. On the night of the program, Bobby bounded up the three steps leading to the chancel and walked unfaltering to center stage. But once he got there, he froze. The director quietly prompted him to recite his poem, and as he scanned the congregation, all he could utter was, "Good Lord—look at all the people!" Not quite the poem he had memorized, but a tribute to the Lord nonetheless.

Sign at a pet store:

FOR SALE:
Christian snake.
Guaranteed to
hate apples.

* * *

When my daughter was about three years old, I took her to bed and asked what she would like to pray about. Promptly she answered: "Onions." I didn't know why she wanted to pray about onions, but I shrugged and we went ahead and prayed about onions. The next morning I asked why she had wanted to pray about onions.

"Because the preacher said in his sermon that we should pray for things we don't like."

Mrs. Donovan was walking down O'Connell Street when she ran into Father Rafferty. "Hello there," he said. "Aren't you Mrs. Donovan, and didn't I marry you and your husband?"

She replied, "Yes, you did, Father."

The priest asked, "And are there any wee ones yet?"

She replied, "No, not yet, Father."

The priest said, "Well now, I'm going to Rome next week; I'll light a candle for you."

"Thank you, Father. That would be wonderful."

They parted ways. Some years later, they met again. The priest asked, "Well now, Mrs. Donovan, how are you these days?"

"Very well, Father," she replied.

He asked, "Tell me, have you been blessed with any wee ones yet?"

"Three sets of twins and four singles," she said. "Ten in all."

"Wonderful!" said the Father. "And how is your husband?"

She replied, "He's gone to Rome to blow out your blasted candle!"

✻ ✻ ✻

Dear Pastor,
I liked your sermon on Sunday. Especially when it was finished.

Marie, age 7

When my daughter Isabel said her bedtime prayers, she would bless every family member, every friend, and every animal she could think of. For several weeks, after we had finished the nightly prayer, Isabel would say, "And all girls."

I asked her, "Isabel, why do you always add the part about all girls?"

Her response was, "Because everybody else always finishes their prayers by saying 'All Men!'"

✻ ✻ ✻

Take the time today to smile at someone who is hard to love. Say hell to someone who doesn't care much about you.

Struggling to make ends meet on a first-call salary, the pastor was livid when he confronted his wife with the receipt for a $250 dress she had bought. "How could you do this?"

"I was outside the store looking at the dress in the window, and suddenly I found myself trying it on," she explained. "It was like Satan was whispering in my ear, 'You look fabulous in that dress. Buy it!'"

"You know how I deal with that kind of temptation. I say, 'Get behind me, Satan!'" said the pastor.

"I did," replied his wife. "But then he said, 'It looks fabulous from back here too!'"

Seen in a wedding program:

What therefore
God has joined together,
let no man sep-
arate.

Wayne and Steve had not seen each other for more than a year when they ran into each other at their church's retreat. Wayne, remembering Steve's wife had been ill, asked how she was. "My wife has gone on to be with Jesus," said Steve.

"Oh, I am so sorry," Wayne replied. "Uh, I mean I am so happy... I mean I am so surprised... of course I am not surprised, what I mean is..."

※ ※ ※

The pastor was preaching a powerful message about heaven and hell, at the end of which he bellowed, "Now, who wants to go to heaven?" Everyone in the small congregation raised their hand, except a wide-eyed boy who was seated down front. The pastor boomed out the question again, but still, the little boy was a holdout. The pastor stepped down from the pulpit and walked over to the child. "Son, don't you want to go to heaven?"

"Sure, Pastor, someday—but not if you're getting up a group today."

During a papal audience, an ad exec approached the pope and made this offer: Change the Lord's Prayer from "Give us this day our daily bread" to "Give us this day our daily chicken," and Kentucky Fried Chicken will donate a million dollars to Catholic charities. The pope declined.

Two weeks later, the man approached the pope again, this time offering $5 million. Again, the pope declined.

A month later, the man upped the price to $25 million, and this time the pope agreed.

At a meeting of the cardinals, the pope announced his decision in the good news/bad news format. "The good news is: We have just earned $25 million for charities. The bad news: We lost the Wonder Bread account."

Madison's family attends a Protestant church, so when she went to Catholic mass with the family of her friend Maria, she poked Maria in the ribs excitedly when the priest came down the aisle wearing his robes and swinging a thurible of incense.

"That man's wearing a dress!" she exclaimed. "And his purse is on fire!"

Heaven: The REAL Gated Community

The team knew what Reverend Oscar expected when he put his hand on the football during the pregame prayer and said, "This too shall pass."

* * *

A little boy was asked why he had left the vegetables on his plate at dinner. "Are you too full? Don't you like them?" his mother asked. The little boy shook his head. "Father Dan taught us in Sunday school that you're supposed to give 10 percent back to the church, so that's their share of my supper."

A devout Christian prays that God will hear his prayers. Sure enough, one night God appears and asks the man what he wants. The man says, "I want peace on earth and also a few million dollars." There's a silence of a few moments and finally God says, "Peace on earth is kind of tough. Maybe you could wish for something else?" And the man thinks for a few seconds too, then says, "Okay. Make it so my wife understands me." And God says, "You want the million dollars first or peace on earth first?"

Jesus fed the masses with just two fish and five loaves of bread. Weary mothers know the real miracle: that there wasn't a child among them who refused the bread unless Jesus cut off the crust.

A middle-aged woman has a heart attack and is taken to the hospital. While on the operating table she has a near-death experience. She sees God and asks, "God, is this it? Am I dying?" God reassures her that she has another 30 years to live.

Upon her recovery she decides to stay in the hospital and have a face-lift, liposuction, breast

augmentation—everything she's always wanted. She even has someone come in to cut and color her hair. She figures that since she's got another 30 years, she might as well make the most of it.

The day the doctors release her, she walks out of the hospital—only to be hit by a speeding ambulance. She arrives in front of God and complains, "I thought you said I had another 30 years!"

"Sorry," God replied. "I didn't recognize you."

❋   ❋   ❋

CHURCH HAPPENINGS

The potholes in the church parking lot will be filled next week. In the meantime, welcome to the holey land.

Pastor Jones and his wife have nine children and one on the way. His hobbies include horses and reading books about breeding.

※ ※ ※

"It is the test of a good
religion whether you
can joke about it."

G. K. CHESTERTON